Contents

Task 1 Make a picture book

Make a picture book.

✿ Draw pictures of yourself as a baby.

✿ Draw yourself two days old.

✿ Put your pictures in a book.

me at 2 days old

✿ Use Task Sheet 1 to make your book.

What babies need

✖ What do babies need?

✖ Draw and write your ideas.

Babies need to be kept clean.

✖ How many ideas did you have?

✖ Share your ideas with others.

Baby food

✺ Find out what foods you ate as a baby.

✺ Draw and write a list.

Babies and toddlers

Two mothers visited Class 2. One brought a 5-month-old baby. The other brought a 2-year-old toddler. The class asked the mothers some questions.

✿ Think of some more questions to ask.

✿ Write them on Task Sheet 2.

Same and different

Class 2 made lists of how the baby and toddler were the same and how they were different.

Same

Baby	Toddler
eats	eats
sleeps	sleeps

Different

Baby	Toddler
cannot walk	can walk or run
cannot speak	can speak

✶ Make your own lists of how babies and toddlers are the same and how they are different.

✶ Use Task Sheet 3.

Task 6 Growing into adults

- Pencil the name of each person on the back of both photos.

- Mix up all the photos in your group.
  Match the adult and the child pictures.

- How has each person changed?

YOU NEED:

one photo of an adult you know

one photo of the same adult as a child

Matching animals

All animals have young. Young animals can grow into adults, then have young themselves.

✳ Cut out the adult animals and their young on Task Sheet 4.

✳ Match the adult to the young animal.

✳ Put them in pairs. Write labels for them.

Class 2 made a collection of different foods and food pictures.

They sorted them into groups using a table.

Foods for activity

1 rice	2	3

⭐ Use Task Sheet 5 to choose foods
for growth, **for health** and **for activity**.

⭐ Cut out, stick and label them in Task Sheet 6.

Food survey

Class 2 planned a survey to find out the
favourite foods in the class.
Each group made a tally chart.
Here is group A's chart.

Food	Number of children tally	Total
biscuits	ⅢⅢ	5
fish fingers	∣	1
samosas	∣∣∣	3

✲ In your groups, plan and carry out your own
survey of favourite foods.

✲ Use Task Sheet 7.

Group A made a block graph on the computer
using their survey results.

10

Our favourite foods

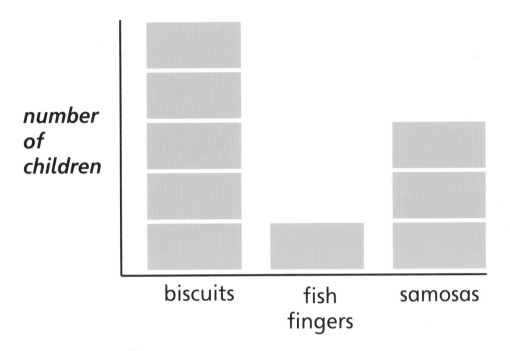

favourite foods

✦ Use your survey results to make your own block graph on Task Sheet 8.

✦ Answer these questions using your graph:
  • How many different favourite foods were there?
  • Which was the favourite food of your group?
  • Which was the least favourite food?

✦ What else does your graph tell you?

Task
10 Party time

Sam is having a birthday party. Help her to plan a party meal for this special day.

✸ Draw and write your ideas for the party food and drink.

✸ Use Task Sheet 9.

✸ Share your ideas with others.

✸ Are they foods and drinks you would have everyday? Why not?

Task 11 Exercise

Class 2 learned how exercise keeps them healthy. They drew and labelled pictures. They showed how they felt before and after a P.E. lesson.

Before P.E.

I feel as though I could run right round the playground. I'm not too hot and not too cold.

After P.E.

I am puffed out. I am hot and my legs feel tired.

✿ Draw and write to show how you feel before P.E. and how you feel after P.E.

✿ List the differences you felt before and after P.E.

✿ Why do you think exercise keeps you healthy?

13

Any questions?

Class 2 talked about medicine and health.
They knew that they were given medicines some-
times when they were poorly. They found out
more about medicines.

⭐ Write your own questions about medicines
and health.

⭐ Use Task Sheet 10.

⭐ Choose two questions to ask the school nurse.

13 Be safe with medicines

✴ Make a poster about how to use medicines safely.

✴ In your group, think about:
  • safe packaging for medicines
  • how to store medicines safely
  • how to take medicines safely.

✴ Plan your poster. Then draw it.

People who take medicine must read the label first.

Medicines should have safety caps.

Keep medicines out of reach of children.

✴ Make a class display of the posters.

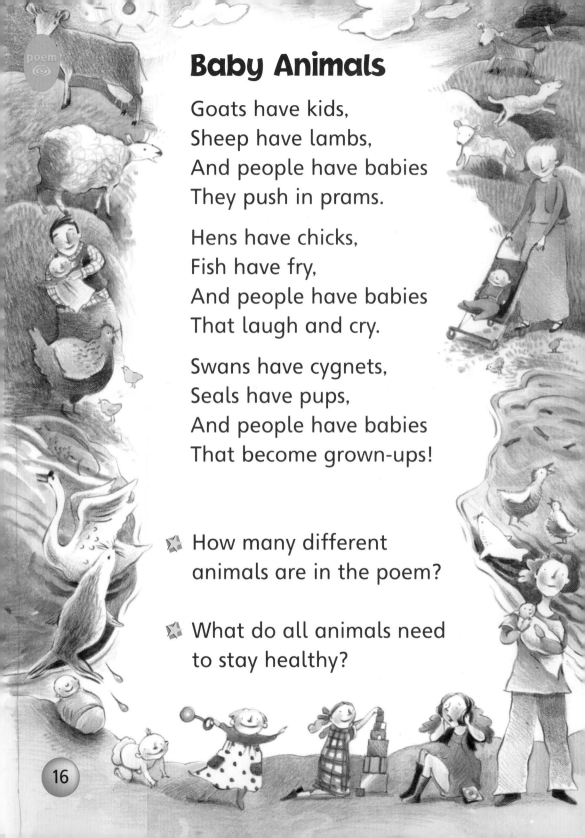

Baby Animals

Goats have kids,
Sheep have lambs,
And people have babies
They push in prams.

Hens have chicks,
Fish have fry,
And people have babies
That laugh and cry.

Swans have cygnets,
Seals have pups,
And people have babies
That become grown-ups!

How many different
animals are in the poem?

What do all animals need
to stay healthy?